Tattooing and Body Piercing

Perspectives on Physical Health

by Bonnie Graves

Consultant:
Robert L. Montagna
Former President/Current Board Member
Alliance of Professional Tattooists, Inc.

LifeMatters
an imprint of Capstone Press
Mankato, Minnesota

LifeMatters Books are published by Capstone Press
PO Box 669 • 151 Good Counsel Drive • Mankato, Minnesota 56002
http://www.capstone-press.com

Printed in the United States of America

Library of Congress Cataloging-in-Publication Data
Graves, Bonnie B.
    Tattooing and body piercing / by Bonnie Graves.
        p.   cm.—(Perspectives on physical health)
    Includes bibliographical references and index.
    Summary: Discusses the history of tattooing and body piercing, the process of each procedure, the risks involved, other options, and tips for making decisions about getting body modification.
    ISBN 0-7368-0417-X (book)—ISBN 0-7368-0438-2 (series)
    1. Tattooing—Juvenile literature. 2. Body piercing—Juvenile literature.
    [1. Tattooing. 2. Body piercing.] I. Title. II. Series.
    GT2345 .G73 2000
    391.6′5—dc21   99-053832
                                              CIP

Staff Credits
Rebecca Aldridge, editor; Adam Lazar, designer; Jodi Theisen, photo researcher

Photo Credits
Cover: PNI/©StockByte
Corbis/Bettmann-UPI/12
FPG International/©Gary Randall, 24
International Stock/©Michael Paras, 59
Photo Network/©Mary E. Messenger, 35
PNI/©RubberBall, 27; ©StockByte, 7, 8, 15, 30, 36, 44
Unicorn Stock Photos/©Jean Higgins, 21; ©Russell R. Grundke, 33; ©Eric R. Berndt, 49; ©Steve Bourgeois, 50; ©Florent Flipper, 53
Uniphoto/©Jessica Inch, 16; ©Scott Suchman, 22; ©Shaun Van Steyn, 41, 58
Visuals Unlimited/©Robert Clay, 43

A 0 9 8 7 6 5 4 3 2 1

Table of Contents

Tattooing and body piercing have been around since ancient times.

A tattoo is a marking or design on the body. It can be permanent or temporary.

Body piercings are holes made in the body in which jewelry is worn.

Choosing to get a tattoo or body piercing is a decision that lasts a lifetime.

In the United States, no federal laws prohibit tattooing or body piercing. However, some states and counties have laws regarding these practices.

Chapter 1

Tattoos and Body Piercings— What Are They?

NIKKI, AGE 16

Nikki and her mom sat at a sidewalk cafe downtown. Nikki enjoyed watching people. So many of them had body jewelry and tattoos. Nikki loved the look but didn't tell her mom this. She knew her mom wouldn't approve. Her mom thought multiple piercings and tattoos were silly, impractical, and dangerous.

Nikki daydreamed about having a pierced belly button. To top off the look, she'd have a butterfly tattooed on her stomach. "How hot would that look with my new crop top?" Nikki thought.

Teens sometimes have friends give them tattoos. Some teens even give themselves one. They may use objects such as pencils, pens, straight pins, or needles. The pigments, or substances used for colors, may include mascara, india ink, carbon, soot, or charcoal. The unclean conditions and types of dyes used increase the chance for infection and risk a person's health.

Body Modification: Trendy but Not New

Tattooing and body piercing are somewhat trendy now. Both gained popularity in the 1990s. However, neither is anything new. They both have been around since ancient times. Tattooing and body piercing are sometimes called body modification. This is because the body is being modified, or changed, in some way. However, while fashions and trends come and go, body modifications last a lifetime.

RICO AND HENRI, AGES 14 AND 15

Rico and Henri gazed in the window of the tattoo parlor.

"Take a look at the cool flash. What do you think of that one?" Rico asked as he pointed.

"The skeleton with the guitar? Definitely," Henri said.

What Is a Tattoo Anyway?

Tattoo is simply the name for a marking or design on the body. The word *tattoo* comes from *tatu,* a Tahitian word that means to mark something. What Rico called flash are tattoo designs. Tattoo shops display flash on their walls. These tattoo designs can be almost anything. They may range from symbols, such as a skull and crossbones, to detailed sketches of flowers or animals.

Tattoos can consist of one color or many. They can be permanent or temporary. Permanent tattoos are made by injecting dye into the second layer of the skin. Temporary tattoos rest on top of the skin, not in it. These temporary designs can be applied with a brush or made with a decal, or color-filled design. This design is pressed against the skin with a moistened sponge.

"I had my eyebrow pierced by a professional piercer named Tasha. **MARIO, AGE 17** She was pretty cool. Tasha told me that she pierced her ears herself when she was 10. Tasha said she was lucky that nothing went wrong.

"Tasha studied with a professional in San Francisco before she opened her own shop. Tasha said, 'Piercers have to know what they're doing. You're talking other people's bodies here.' I'm glad I went to a professional like Tasha. I'm happy with the piercing job she did for me."

What Is Body Piercing?

Body piercings are holes made in the body. Jewelry of some kind is placed through the holes. The earlobe and the elastic tissue of the outside ear, or ear cartilage, are the most frequently pierced sites. Other piercing sites include the lip, tongue, nose, eyebrow, nipple, and navel. Some people pierce their genitals, or sex organs. For example, men may pierce their penis, and women may pierce their labia.

Some people do not think of body piercings as permanent. In some areas of the body, the tissue grows back if the jewelry is removed. However, a scar usually remains.

Body Modification and Teens

Tattooing is gaining interest among teens. In a 1995 study, about 9 percent of high school teens had tattoos. In the same study, 55 percent of high school teens expressed interest in tattooing. Still, more than 90 percent of teens choose not to tattoo.

Not much research is available on teens and body piercing. However, school nurses are reporting more health problems caused by piercings on various body parts. Teens who choose piercing tend to limit it to their earlobes.

Samuel O'Reilly patented the first electronic tattoo machine in 1891. This machine made tattooing more affordable for the public.

Currently in the United States, there are no federal laws against tattooing or piercing minors. In many states, tattooing or body piercing anyone under age 18 without parental consent is illegal. In fact, tattooing is against the law in several states.

What About You?

Maybe you're thinking about getting a body piercing. Maybe you are considering a tattoo. You may like the look and want to be part of the trend. It is important to give such a decision careful thought. The choice you make will be with you for a lifetime.

Points to Consider

Do you like the look of tattoos? Why or why not?

Why do you think teens find body piercings appealing?

Do you think the trend in tattooing and body piercing will last? Why or why not?

Why shouldn't a person get tattooed or pierced on the spur of the moment?

Chapter
Overview

Chapter
Overview

The history of tattooing and body piercing goes back through the centuries.

Today, people get tattooed and pierced for a variety of reasons. Some of these reasons are similar to those of the past.

Tattooing is sometimes used for cosmetic medical reasons or permanent makeup.

Teens choose to modify their bodies for different reasons. Some teens may want to make a fashion statement, identify with a certain group, or rebel against mainstream culture.

Chapter **2**

Body Modification, Past and Present

A young Arapaho woman waited to be tattooed. Like the

NATANE, AGE 19

other women in her tribe, she would be tattooed with a single circle on her forehead. She knew the process because she had watched others before her. The skin was pricked with cactus spines. Powdered charcoal was then rubbed into the punctures, or holes. When the punctures healed, a sort of magic happened. The tattoo became as blue as the sky.

As mentioned previously, tattooing and body piercing have been practiced for centuries. They have been practiced in many cultures as well. These cultures vary from the ancient Egyptians to 17th- and 18th-century Polynesians. Recently, a 4,000-year-old tattooed man was discovered in a glacier in Austria.

Tattooing in the Past

Over the centuries, tattooing was done for many different reasons. For example, the Japanese in 500 B.C. tattooed for cosmetic, decorative, and religious reasons. They also used tattoos to identify and punish criminals. In the late 1800s, tattoos were quite fashionable among England's royalty. In fact, Winston Churchill's mother, Lady Randolf Churchill, had a snake tattooed around her wrist.

Until recently, in the United States, tattoos often were considered a macho thing. Sailors, gang members, and motorcyclists were among those who had tattoos. Many people considered tattoo shops dangerous and socially unacceptable.

In the Middle Ages, people in Europe believed that demons could enter the body through the left ear. Men wore earrings to keep these demons away.

Body Piercing in the Past

Like tattooing, body piercing also has been practiced a long time. Its history, however, doesn't go back quite as far as that of tattooing. One source credits the 2nd-century Romans as one of the first groups to practice body piercing.

As with tattooing, body piercing has been practiced in many cultures and for many different reasons. For example, Egyptian pharaohs pierced their navels as a rite of passage. This symbolized their change in status. Roman soldiers pierced their nipples to show their manhood. Mayans pierced their tongues as a spiritual ritual. And, of course, some people pierced their earlobes strictly to be fashionable.

Tattooing and Body Piercing Today

People today get tattooed and pierced for a variety of reasons. Some reasons are similar to those of the past. Some people get a tattoo to show loyalty to a certain group. For example, gang members might get a tattoo that signifies allegiance to their gang. Members of the military might choose tattoos that represent their branch of service.

Branding is another form of body modification. In branding, a white-hot metal shape is pressed into the flesh. The portion of flesh struck becomes a scar. The result is a raised design on the skin. One design must be done in sections, so the skin is actually branded several times. Branding is not as popular as tattooing, but the trend is growing. Like tattooing, it comes with its own set of risks.

Beginning in the 1980s, the popularity of both tattooing and body piercing increased. Men started piercing their ears. Multiple ear piercings became common for both women and men. Tattoos of roses or butterflies began appearing on ankles and shoulders. Tattooed and pierced celebrities have helped the fad along. These people are highly visible. They are like walking advertisements for body art. Cher, Dennis Rodman, and Pamela Anderson Lee are just a few celebrities who have been tattooed.

TARA, AGE 18

Tara had very light eyebrows. She was tired of buying eyebrow pencils. She was even more tired of using them every morning. She had to, though. If she didn't, she looked like some sort of eyebrowless space creature. Tara had read about eyebrow tattoos. She wondered if this would be a good idea for her.

Tattooing and Body Piercing

Recently, tattoos have come into use for both medical and nonmedical cosmetic reasons. Tattooing is used to cover up port-wine stains on a person's face. These are reddish purple birthmarks. Tattooing also is used to color the skin of people with vitiligo. This is a disorder in which the skin loses its pigment. Tattooing also can be used for permanent makeup such as eyeliner.

"When I was 11, I wanted my ears pierced in the worst way. **JOSLYN, AGE 19** Both my older sisters had pierced ears. Many of my friends did, too. But my mom said, 'No, you can't have pierced ears until you are 14.' For three years, I fought with my mom about it, but she never gave in. Finally, I turned 14 and the strangest thing happened. I no longer wanted my ears pierced. It didn't matter to me anymore. I'm 19 now, and I still don't have pierced ears. I kind of like being different."

Attraction of Teens to Tattooing and Body Piercing

Teens get tattoos and piercings for many different reasons. A teen may be making a statement about who he or she is. To a certain person, tattoos and body jewelry might say one or more of the following:

"Look at me."

"I'm a risk taker."

"I'm mature."

"I'm part of this group."

"I like to wear art on my body."

"I'm fashionable, cool, and hip."

A person's hairstyle, makeup, jewelry, and clothing all say something about him or her. The same goes for tattoos and body piercings. For some teens, tattoos and body piercings are a fashion statement. Teens who have tattoos or piercings may hope to express their individuality through them.

Why did you get a body piercing?

"I'm into art. Piercing is just a form of body art."
—Kendra, age 18

"It's fashionable, that's all."—Dion, age 15

"It makes a personal statement."—Jacq, age 16

"It makes me feel daring, like I'm doing something different."—Kelly, age 17

Other teens may want body modification in order to be identified with a certain group. Some may get tattooed or pierced to rebel against parents' values or mainstream culture. Still others may choose tattoos or piercings to be like older brothers, sisters, friends, or celebrities that they admire.

Points to Consider

Were you surprised to learn body modification has been around a long time? Why or why not?

Why do you think tattooing and body piercing have become trendier in recent years?

Why do you think some teens find the idea of tattoos appealing?

Do you think people who have tattoos or body piercings present a certain image? Explain.

A professional tattooist is someone who has studied the art of tattooing and who uses safe tattooing practices.

The cost of a tattoo varies according to the artist and the size of the design.

The tattooing procedure includes several steps. The site is cleaned and prepared. Then the design is traced, outlined, and filled in.

Taking proper care of a fresh tattoo is necessary to prevent infection and to allow proper healing.

Today, tattoos can be removed with lasers. This is an expensive procedure and is not 100 percent successful. Also, tattoos can be covered up with other tattoos or with special makeup.

Chapter **3**

Getting a Tattoo and Getting Rid of It

"Does it hurt?" Koko asked Spider. Spider was a tattoo artist that Koko had met at a party.

"It depends. The kind of skin you have matters. So does your tolerance for pain. For some people, getting a tattoo hurts a lot. Other people barely feel it. Are you thinking of getting a tattoo?" Spider asked.

"Yeah," Koko said.

"Come by my studio sometime. I can show you what it's all about."

The Alliance of Professional Tattooists (APT) is a nonprofit organization. Together with the FDA, it has developed a set of infection control guidelines for tattooists to follow.

The Professional Tattooist

Spider is a professional tattooist. A professional tattooist is someone who has studied the art of tattooing and uses safe tattooing practices. Spider learned the art of tattooing from a master tattooist. Spider keeps on top of his profession by attending body modification conferences. He also belongs to the Alliance of Professional Tattooists (APT). This group promotes standards that help reduce health risks.

A certificate hangs on the wall in Spider's studio. It proves he has completed a course in cleanliness and sterilization techniques. That means his studio is clean and germ-free. Spider is proud that his shop uses the most up-to-date sterilization procedures. At his studio, Spider follows these APT guidelines:

Has an autoclave; this is a heat sterilization machine regulated by the Food and Drug Administration (FDA).

Has customers fill out consent forms before tattooing begins

Washes and dries hands immediately before tattooing

Wears latex gloves at all times during tattooing

Uses only autoclaved needle bars and tubes on each customer

Cleans all surfaces that can't be autoclaved with a disinfectant, or a chemical that kills germs

Disposes of used tissues in a special leak-proof container

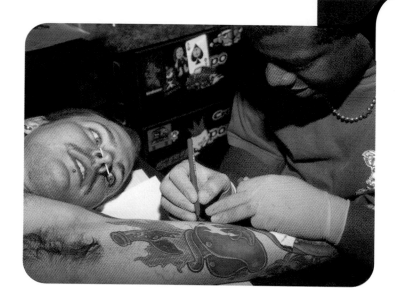

How Much Does a Tattooist Charge?

Tattoo prices vary. The average cost of a small tattoo is about $45. A larger design usually costs about $200. However, some tattooists charge more than others do. Some of the best tattooists may charge at a rate of about $200 per hour.

How a Tattoo Is Made

After washing his or her hands, the tattooist puts on latex gloves. Then he or she inspects the client's skin to make sure there are no cuts or scrapes. The skin is sprayed with an antiseptic to kill germs and prevent infection. The hairs in the area are shaved. Razors used for shaving are disposed of immediately in a special container.

The tattooist begins by stenciling or tracing the design on the skin. A stencil is a single-use sheet. It is used to transfer the chosen image or design to the site to be tattooed. After the stenciling or tracing, the tattooist spreads a layer of ointment over the area to be tattooed. Petroleum jelly is one type of ointment that may be used.

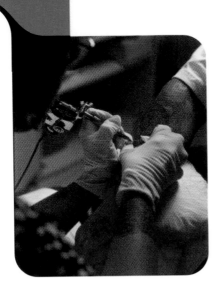

Next, the tattooist uses the tattooing machine to outline and shade the design. First, the outline is made with a needle bar that has three to five needles connected to it. The needle bar is inserted into a tube and then into the tattoo machine. The skin is slightly numb by the time outlining is complete.

Filling in with a shader comes next. A shader is a needle bar with 5 to 13 flat needles or 5 to 7 round needles. It is used to shade in and color the tattoo.

The tattooing machine works like a mini-sewing machine. The needle bar moves up and down to inject the tattoo dye 3,000 times per minute. The tattooist controls the speed of the machine with a knob on the power pack. This power pack is located away from the machine and the foot switch that turns the machine on and off. The dye goes into the second layer of the skin at a depth of $\frac{1}{64}$ to $\frac{1}{16}$ of an inch.

The tattooist guides the tattoo machine over the skin. He or she stops the needle every minute or so to wipe the blood and ink clean. The amounts of bleeding and pain in the tattoo process differ according to each person.

Places you definitely do not want to go to get a tattoo:

A garage

An apartment

A tent at a circus

A music festival

A motorcycle shop

The time it takes to get a tattoo varies. Small tattoos usually can be done in an hour. Larger tattoos can take several hours. Some even need to be done in more than one sitting. A person getting a tattoo may only want to sit a few hours at a time. The tattooist may only want to work a few hours at a time on a large tattoo.

JORDAN, AGE 15

Jordan's tattoo took about two hours to complete. He was glad when the process was over. He was nervous and felt a bit odd the whole time. It hurt more than he thought it would, and the buzzing of the tattoo machine made him uncomfortable. Jordan whispered to his mom that he didn't think he'd be back for a second tattoo for a while.

Aftercare

A tattoo needs to be cared for after it has been completed. When a tattoo is finished, the tattooed area is washed with mild soap and water. Then the area is covered with an antiseptic ointment and a gauze bandage. All reputable tattooists give their clients detailed aftercare instructions.

Here are the most basic aftercare guidelines:

Use soap and water to keep the area clean.

After the first two hours, remove the bandage and wash away any collected or dried blood.

Apply mild lotion or vitamin A and D ointment to the area for the first five to seven days. Then use a mild hand cream to keep the tattooed area moist until healing is complete.

Avoid exposure to direct sunlight for the first four weeks.

Until the peeling stops, avoid hot tubs, swimming pools, and hot baths. These can ruin a tattoo.

Caring for a tattoo is like caring for a minor burn. The tattoo should be kept clean and moist. The tattooed skin scabs, crusts slightly, and peels. This is part of the healing process. Initial healing usually takes 10 days to 2 weeks. A tattoo may take longer to heal completely for some people.

Tattoo removal programs exist for gang members who want out. A program in Dallas, Texas, called D-TAG helps teen gang members get out of gang life by sponsoring their tattoo removal. The Salt Lake City Area Gang Project also offers free tattoo removal for former gang members.

Getting Rid of Tattoos

People who get tattoos sometimes decide they no longer want them. A tattoo that looked great in high school may look out of place in the business world. A gang tattoo is undesirable when a person leaves the gang. A tattoo that reads *Tina* is not so great for the guy who marries Lindsay.

Tattoo removal is possible, but it is difficult and expensive. It's not always successful, either. Skin pigment can be lost. Scarring takes place, too. In the past, tattoos were sometimes removed by destroying the first and second layers of skin. One way to do this was to sand the skin with a wire brush. Another way was to let a salt solution soak into the skin. A third way was to use an acid solution. All three methods caused pain and scarring.

Today lasers are used to remove tattoos. A laser is a device that makes a narrow and powerful beam of light that can cut things. The lasers used for tattoo removal get rid of most color with little scarring. This process is expensive and is not always 100 percent successful. Sometimes it is impossible to get the skin color back after removing a tattoo.

"Asking a friend to give you a tattoo can ruin a friendship. This happened to me. I gave my friend Walker the tattoo I thought he wanted. It didn't turn out the way he thought it would. He hasn't talked to me since."—Geoff, age 16

"Fads come and go, but tattoos stay."—Helena, age 14

Some people hide their tattoo rather than remove it. Some people choose to "remove" a tattoo by hiding it with another one. The second tattoo is larger than the first. It hides the first tattoo within the new design's colors and shapes. Another option for hiding a tattoo is to use a special waterproof makeup. This technique can be used to temporarily cover a tattoo.

CHEN, AGE 19

Chen got a tattoo on his arm a couple of years ago. Now he is embarrassed by it. He hardly ever wears short-sleeve shirts, and he rarely goes to the beach. When Chen read about a makeup used by burn victims, he asked his doctor about it. She located some of the makeup for Chen. Now Chen uses the foundation on some occasions. It allows him to feel more comfortable in public.

Points to Consider

Why should a person choose a professional tattooist?

Which part of the tattooing process do you think is most critical? Why?

Why do you think someone might want to get rid of a tattoo?

What are some reasons that a teen might regret a tattoo later in life?

Chapter
Overview

Body piercing should only be done by a professional and only in sterile, or germ-free, conditions.

The style of jewelry worn depends on the body part pierced. Jewelry should be made of a hypoallergenic metal.

Carefully following aftercare instructions is critical to avoid infection.

A piercing grows out if jewelry is not worn. However, a permanent mark or scar usually remains.

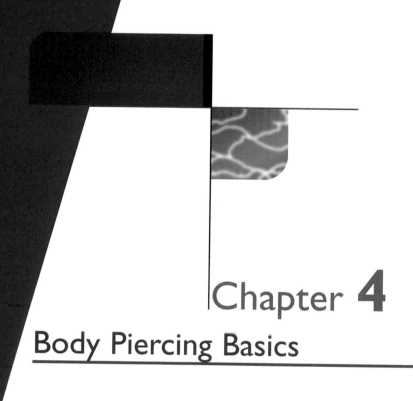

Chapter **4**

Body Piercing Basics

The Professional Piercer

All piercings should be done by a professional. Professionals follow strict rules. One of those rules involves piercing minors. Most professionals will not pierce anyone under the age of 18, except for piercing the earlobes. In many cases, a parent must be present even for earlobe piercing. Some professionals will body pierce 16- and 17-year-olds. However, this happens only if the teen has proper identification and a parent present. In some states, law forbids the piercing of anyone under age 18 without a parent's consent.

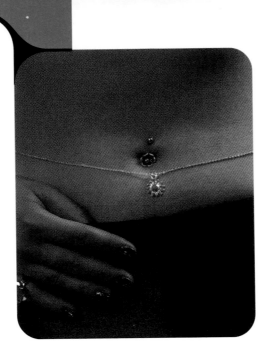

Professional piercers know what sites can be pierced and how to pierce them. Professionals also follow all procedures for proper sterilization.

The piercer had just clamped Chandra's navel when the phone rang. "Will she answer it?" Chandra wondered.

"Oh, darn," her piercer, Renee, said. "Sorry, but I've got to answer that. Hang tight. I'll be right back."

Chandra noticed Renee didn't take off her latex gloves. When she came back into the room, she was still wearing them. Chandra had read about the infections you could pick up getting pierced. She certainly didn't want to get any of them. Renee's shop looked clean. She had an autoclave. Chandra wondered if she had used it on the clamp. Chandra also wondered if Renee would put on a new pair of gloves. Suddenly, Chandra felt nervous.

Chandra had every right to feel nervous. She knew piercers should wear latex gloves. She also knew that if the piercer was interrupted during the procedure, new gloves needed to be worn. The following are important guidelines body piercers should follow:

Have an autoclave

Presterilize and store instruments and supplies in sterile bags

Use only needles from sterile packages

Use needles only once and discard them in a biohazard container. These containers keep people from being exposed to hazardous material.

Have customers fill out consent forms before piercing begins

Wash and dry hands immediately before piercing

Wear a fresh pair of latex gloves at all times during piercing

Disinfect all instruments and supplies that cannot be autoclaved

Use only autoclaved, hypoallergenic jewelry. This type of jewelry is not likely to cause an allergic reaction.

Clean and disinfect the premises frequently

A piercing gun should be used only on the earlobes. It should not be used on any other areas of the body. On these areas, it crushes the tissues that are pierced.

Going to a professional who works in sterile conditions lessens the health risks of piercing. These risks are discussed in the next chapter.

DEVON, AGE 17

Devon wanted to get his nose pierced. He'd been thinking about it for a long time. His friends had recommended the PinPoint Studio on Grand Street. Devon talked with his dad, and his dad agreed to take him. Devon made an appointment for Saturday morning.

At the studio, the piercer, Mark, checked Devon's driver's license. Then Mark explained the entire piercing procedure to Devon. Next he gave Devon a release-and-consent form to sign. This form makes sure the customer is aware of the process, aftercare, and possible effects involved. It also serves as positive identification of the customer and as a birth-date check.

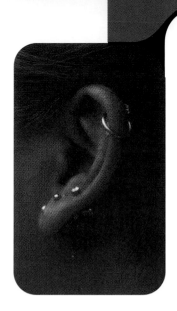

Cost

The piercing procedure alone can cost between $20 and $60, depending on the site pierced. Jewelry is an added expense. Jewelry in the recommended hypoallergenic metals begins at about $35. This second cost is sometimes unexpected because a person may assume the price given includes the jewelry. A piercing and one piece of jewelry may range from $55 to $110.

How Piercing Is Done

Professional piercers follow several steps during a piercing. First, the piercer cleans the area to be pierced with a disinfectant. Then, two dots are drawn. One dot marks the spot where the needle will enter the body. The other dot indicates where the needle will exit. If necessary, the area to be pierced is clamped. Navel piercings require a surgical clamp. The clamp pulls the skin to be pierced away from the rest of the body.

The piercer inserts a hollow needle through the body part. The size of the needle used depends on the body part being pierced. The jewelry is attached to the needle. Once the hole is made, the jewelry is quickly pushed through.

What would you recommend to others about body piercing?

"You need to follow the guidelines the piercer gives you. I slacked off and got an infection."—Latrel, age 17

"It's tempting, but don't play with your jewelry."
—Nadya, age 15

"Go to a studio. A friend did my piercing. It wasn't deep enough, and it got infected."—Kris, age 16

"Don't use alcohol to clean your navel piercing."
—Sarah, age 18

Jewelry

The style of jewelry used depends on the body part pierced. Jewelry can range from small to large hoops to barbell-type studs. A barbell is a straight cylinder that is capped at both ends with a detachable ball. The jewelry used should accommodate the swelling that occurs after the piercing. Jewelry, like all the equipment used in a piercing, is autoclaved before it is placed through the hole.

Piercers recommend jewelry in hypoallergenic metals. This is to help prevent infections and allergic reactions. Two good choices are surgical steel and 14-karat gold. Other metals such as sterling silver should not be worn in fresh piercings. They can cause infection and slow healing.

Aftercare

The area around a new piercing must be kept clean. All reputable piercers will give their customers proper care instructions. Instructions are somewhat varied for the different areas pierced. For example, caring for a pierced navel is different from caring for pierced ears. These are some general guidelines for the care of new piercing sites:

Wash the piercing area with an antibacterial soap twice a day. Remove all crusty formations from the piercing site and jewelry. Rinse away all soap and crust formations. Do not use alcohol to clean the piercing site.

Always wash hands with antibacterial soap before touching any piercing.

Spin or twist jewelry only during cleaning.

Avoid contact with other people's body fluids.

After exercise, rinse the area to remove all sweat.

Wear clean clothes.

Avoid contact with nonsterile items.

Avoid public pools and hot tubs until the piercing has healed.

Healing times for piercings vary. The chart below shows average healing times.

Healing Times for Body Piercings	
Earlobe	6 to 8 weeks
Ear cartilage	4 months to 1 year
Eyebrow	6 to 8 weeks
Nostril	2 to 4 months
Nasal septum	6 to 8 months
Nasal bridge	8 to 10 weeks
Tongue	4 weeks
Lip	2 to 3 months
Nipple	3 to 6 months
Navel	4 months to 1 year
Female genitalia	4 to 10 weeks
Male genitalia	4 weeks to 6 months

LaVon was tired of his lip
piercing. When he first got it, he
thought it was fantastic. He knew it made him look ultra
cool. Knowing it was there gave him a lot of satisfaction.
Then he met Carla. She had other ideas. Carla told LaVon he
had sexy lips, but the jewelry got in the way. She urged him
not to wear it.

LaVon, Age 18

Changing Your Mind

You may wonder what happens if you change your mind. Will the
skin that has been pierced close up? Will there be a scar? There
are no certain answers. Some piercings that grow out leave little
white bumps called keloids on the skin. Some piercings leave no
more than a small dent on the skin. Some leave a scar.

Points to Consider

Why should a professional piercer do all body piercings?

Can any type of jewelry be worn in a piercing? Why or
why not?

Why should a person with a new piercing avoid public
pools?

Do you think people who forget to clean their contact
lenses would be good candidates for body piercing? Why
or why not?

Chapter Overview

Tattooing and body piercing have their health risks. These include hepatitis B and C, HIV and AIDS, tetanus, allergic reactions, and infection.

Body modification also has emotional and social risks. People who get tattoos or body piercings may later regret having done so. They also risk being hurt by others' prejudices regarding body art.

Professional organizations help protect tattooists and piercers and their customers.

Chapter 5

Risks of Tattooing and Body Piercing

"I've heard you can get HIV from getting pierced or tattooed," Mia told Rand. "Aren't you worried about that?"

RAND, AGE 15

"Naw. That's a bunch of bull," Rand said.

"Have you checked it out?" Mia asked.

"No, I've just never heard of anyone getting HIV from a tattoo."

In 1961, there was an outbreak of hepatitis in the United States. This disease of the blood causes inflammation of the liver. The outbreak resulted in a ban on tattooing in many parts of the United States.

Health Risks of Tattooing

Tattooing has had a bad reputation in the recent past. It has even been banned in some states and cities for health and safety reasons. Sanitary, or healthy, conditions are better today, but still there are risks.

Tattooing poses health risks because the process exposes blood and body fluids. Because of this, a person who gets tattooed risks getting a disease or infection that is carried through blood. These blood-borne diseases include hepatitis B and C, tetanus, and HIV. No cases of HIV from tattooing are known to have happened in the United States. However, it could happen. The tattooist needs to carefully follow the infection control practices listed in chapter 3. This reduces the risk of spreading these diseases. Also to reduce the risk of disease, never give yourself a tattoo or let a friend give you one.

Infections and allergic reactions also are risks of tattooing. A person who gets tattooed must follow the aftercare instructions. Failure to do so can cause serious infection. An allergic reaction also can occur with tattoos. Some people are allergic to the tattoo dye. Their body works to reject the tattoo. The result is pain, swelling, and infection.

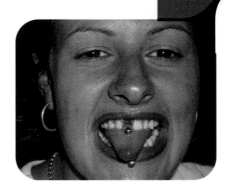

Body Piercing Risks

Body piercing also has its own set of possible problems. As with tattooing, piercing involves breaking the skin. The skin is one of the body's main protective barriers. The major health risks are hepatitis B and C, tetanus, HIV, allergic reaction, and infection.

Piercing the skin risks infection of the piercing site. This can cause a deformity, or blemish, and a scar. Infections can result from a piercing done in unsanitary conditions. This is one reason why you never want to pierce your own body or let a friend do it. Even piercings done in sanitary conditions can become infected. This can happen because of improper aftercare.

Another risk is that jewelry may irritate other parts of the body. A nose piercing may irritate the upper lip. Bottom-lip jewelry may rub against the gum line. This can wear away the gum and cause tooth loss. Also, clothing irritates navel piercings. Waistbands and tight-fitting clothing do not allow air circulation. Moisture collects because of this, and infections can form.

Tongue piercings have their share of problems. For one, the tongue swells after it is pierced. This makes talking difficult. Also, tongue piercings are likely to get infected because the mouth is full of germs. Broken teeth are another hazard. This can happen when the person accidentally bites down on a mouth stud. Swallowing a stud is a risk, too.

Keloids are scar tissue that can develop around piercings. They look like white bumps or rings around a piercing. Some people are more likely than others to get keloids.

Leon wore a 14-karat gold bolt in his tongue pierce. One day he bit down on it. He bit the wrong way and too hard. The bolt sheared off his front tooth. His dentist had to perform surgery. It was an unpleasant procedure that took three visits. It also cost a lot of money.

LEON, AGE 18

Other risks of piercing include:

- Nerve damage and paralysis from improperly placed piercings

- Elongated, or extended, holes from heavy earrings

- Injuries from jewelry getting caught in other objects

- Rejection of jewelry by the body that causes the body to expel the jewelry like a splinter

Professional Organizations Help Minimize Health Risks

Professional tattooists and piercers have organized to protect themselves and their customers. These organizations are the Alliance of Professional Tattooists, Inc. (APT), the National Tattoo Association (NTA), and the Association of Professional Piercers (APP). The APP certifies members, who follow strict safety and health requirements. These three groups promote standards that help minimize the health risks of tattooing and piercing.

Emotional and Social Risks of Body Modification

Most experts believe there is little risk to a person's health if appropriate disinfection and sterilization techniques are used. However, there are emotional and social risks to be aware of with body modification.

Emotional risks include negative feelings you might have as a result of getting a tattoo or piercing. Social risks are those that could change your relationship with others, including friends, parents, teachers, and employers. This includes the people in your life today and those who will be in your life in the future. For example, body modification can affect your chances for future employment. Certain jobs are not available to people who have visible body art.

Maria was invited to meet Jeff's parents at their beach house.

She wanted to make a good impression. However, one thing worried her—the tattoo on her shoulder. What would they think of it? Or worse, what would they think of her for having one?

Maria had gotten the tattoo when she was 16, years before she met Jeff. She hung out with a different crowd back then. When she was 16 she loved that tattoo. Getting one seemed like a good idea at the time. It made her feel sexy and unique. Now she wasn't so sure. What would Jeff's parents think of her when they saw it? And, of course they would see it. How could they not? How could she spend a weekend at the beach and not put on a bathing suit?

Because a tattoo is a lifetime commitment, a person who gets one risks feeling regret. That regret might happen right away or it could happen later. When Maria got her tattoo, she didn't think about the social risks. She wasn't thinking about a future boyfriend or his parents. She wasn't thinking about other people's prejudices about body art.

Myth: If I let my piercing grow out, it won't be noticeable at all.

Fact: There is no way to tell what the skin will look like if you let a piercing grow out.

If you are considering body art, it is important to ask yourself the following questions:

Are you sure the tattoo will look the way you want it to? A permanent tattoo is there to stay.

Will you feel the same way about your tattoo 5 or 10 years from now?

How will other people feel about your tattoo or body piercing? Will you care if they don't like it? How will other people treat you?

Points to Consider

What are some of the risks of getting a tattoo or piercing in unsanitary conditions?

How do you think most people view tattooing and body piercing?

If you were planning to get a tattoo, what would be your greatest fear and why?

Do you think some people have automatic impressions about people who are tattooed or pierced? Explain.

How could body art keep a person from getting a job?

Chapter
Overview

Before making a decision about body modification, it is a good idea to talk with others. Ask people you know about their tattooing or body piercing experiences. Also, ask them if they would do anything differently.

Before making a decision, it is important to get the facts about the risks of tattooing and body piercing.

Someone considering a tattoo or body piercing should make a list of the advantages and disadvantages.

There are nonpermanent options to tattooing and body piercing.

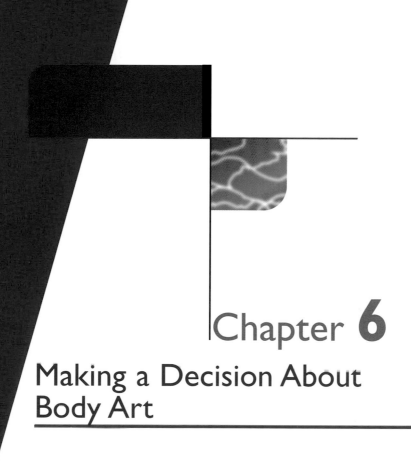

Chapter **6**

Making a Decision About Body Art

Check With Others

Are you thinking about getting a body piercing or tattoo? First, talk with people who have done it. Ask what their experiences have been. Ask them if they would do anything differently if they had to do it again.

Before tattooing or piercing your body, it is a good idea to:

Talk with others who have done it.

Find out the risks involved.

List the pros and cons.

Consider other options.

CARLY, AGE 17

"Your eyebrow pierce is really cool. Do you like it?" Toshi asked.

"Yeah, but want to hear something weird? People treat me differently since I got it. I mean, I've sensed negative reactions. It's kind of annoying," Carly said.

"I thought you got your tongue pierced, too," Toshi said.

"Yeah, but it didn't work for me. So I got rid of the barbell."

"Why?" asked Toshi.

"I got tired of people looking at me funny when I talked. My speech sounded different with the piercing."

Do Your Homework

Before making any decision, it is important to get all the facts you can about body art. Knowing the answers to the following questions can help you make a wise decision.

What are the health risks?

What problems could happen during or after the procedure?

How can the health risks be reduced?

What are the social risks?

How can these social risks be reduced?

What are the emotional risks?

What is the best way to reduce the emotional risks?

How much money will it cost?

How long does the procedure take?

What is the expected healing time?

Who are the professional piercers and tattooists in your area?

What sort of credentials, or qualifications, do these professionals have?

Erik is thinking of getting a tattoo. It's something he has wanted to do for a long time. Erik asked his football coach what he thought of the idea. Coach Brown suggested that Erik sit down and list the pros and cons. Here's the list Erik came up with:

PROS	CONS
The design will look cool.	It's expensive, and I could put the money toward a new mountain bike instead.
The rest of the team will respect me for it.	Someone I want to date in the future may not like it.
It will be like having art on my arm.	Dad will get upset.
It'll let people know that I'm not a wimp.	It could get infected.
	My teachers might treat me differently.

Weigh the Pros and Cons

Writing down lists of advantages and disadvantages can be a good idea. For example, you may be thinking of piercing your navel. If so, you should try writing down all the reasons you want a navel piercing. These are the advantages. Then list some of the problems a navel piercing could cause. These are the disadvantages.

Look carefully at your lists. Do the advantages outweigh the disadvantages? If the answer is yes, then you likely will feel good about getting your navel pierced. This may be the right decision for you. If the disadvantages outweigh the advantages, you may want to wait to get a piercing.

Consider Other Options

There are options to permanent tattoos and body piercings. These options don't have the risks permanent options do. You may feel unsure about committing yourself to the pain and possible complications of tattooing and body piercing. If so, you may want to consider temporary tattoos, painted tattoos, Mehndi, or clip-on or magnetic jewelry.

What was your experience with body piercing?

"I went to a professional. I tried really hard to keep my navel piercing clean. Still, it was sore, red, and had drainage for a long time."
—Thea, age 14

"My nose pierce never did heal right. I eventually had to take out the jewelry and let it close. I felt like I wasted a lot of money for nothing."—Xavier, age 15

"I love having my ears pierced. I've never had problems."
—Jana, age 13

Temporary and Painted Tattoos

Temporary tattoos are available in many novelty, record, book, or magazine shops. They come in many different designs and colors. Temporary tattoos can be placed anywhere on your skin. Then you blot the decal with a moistened rag or sponge. The color and design transfer onto your skin. The result looks much like a real tattoo.

Also, there are kits for painting tattoos. The movie industry uses this method to create realistic-looking tattoos for actors. Both temporary and painted tattoos allow you to experiment with design and placement. Trying either of these tattoo types may help you decide if you really want a permanent tattoo.

Mehndi

Another temporary option to tattooing is Mehndi. With this method, henna is used to dye or tint the skin with a design. Henna is a reddish brown dye that comes from the henna plant. The dye usually remains on the skin for a month or longer. Mehndi designs can be just as intricate as needle-applied tattoos.

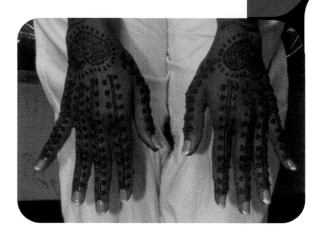

Clip-on and Magnetic Jewelry

Clip-on and magnetic jewelry are options to piercing. Clip-on earrings have been around a long time. Now navel and nose clip-ons are available as well. Magnetic jewelry is another option. The two parts of this jewelry attach with a strong magnet. Magnetic jewelry is available for the upper ear, nose, and lip. Clip-on and magnetic jewelry can achieve the look you want without the pain and expense of an actual piercing.

Points to Consider

How might talking with friends about their tattoo or body piercing experiences help in making your own decision?

What do you think is the most important thing to do before getting a tattoo or body piercing? Explain.

Make lists of what you think are the advantages and disadvantages of tattooing. Make two more lists for body piercing. How do the advantages compare to the disadvantages for each?

What are some of the advantages temporary tattoos have over permanent ones?

Chapter
Overview

Choose the placement of your tattoo or body piercing carefully. This is a lifetime commitment.

Choose a professional to do your tattoo or body piercing. The professional you choose should be someone you feel comfortable with and can trust. He or she also should be certified by the APT or APP.

It's okay to change your mind about getting a tattoo or piercing—even at the last minute.

Chapter 7
Preparing for Body Modification

Choose the Body Site Carefully

It's important to carefully choose what you want on your body. It also is just as important to decide where you want to put a piercing or tattoo. Do you want your body art to be visible or hidden? Some types of body art, such as that which appears on the face, is seen by everyone. A person who chooses visible body art should be prepared. Some people may react negatively to such body modification. Such people as employers may not approve of body art.

Concealed piercings, such as those of the navel, may cause problems, too. These sites may take longer to heal because clothing can irritate them.

"If you get a tattoo, choose one to please yourself—not someone else. Relationships end. I got a tattoo for my boyfriend. Now he's long gone, and unfortunately I still have that tattoo. I wish I could get rid of it. It's an unpleasant reminder of a bad relationship."—Jessica, age 18

Choose the Design Carefully

With tattoos, picking a design also is an important decision. A design choice says something about you and will say it for the rest of your life. A good tattoo artist can help you with both design and placement. He or she should know which designs work well and on which parts of the body. This is another good reason to select a professional artist and studio.

A reputable artist will gladly sketch your design choice on the location you choose. If you don't like the way it looks there, it can be washed off and sketched again somewhere else. It is essential to be happy with both the design of the tattoo and its placement. A tattoo is a lifelong investment. Therefore, it is a good idea not to hurry a decision about design or placement.

LISA, AGE 14

Lisa wanted her navel pierced. A professional piercer wouldn't do it for her. Lisa was too young. She had to have a parent's consent, and her mother wouldn't give it to her. That didn't stop Lisa, though. She wanted her navel pierced in the worst way. She talked her friend, Maddie, into piercing her navel for her. Maddie tried her best but couldn't get the needle in deeply enough. Lisa tried wearing the jewelry for a while, but her body rejected it and pushed it out. The piercing got infected and left a scar.

QUOTE

Choose a Professional and Choose Carefully

Piercings or tattoos done by nonprofessionals can be dangerous. All body piercings and tattoos need to be done by professionals and in sterile conditions. Professionals have strict rules for cleanliness.

Here are some guidelines to help you find the right professional for your body art:

Visit several shops. Take a parent or friend along with you.

Talk with the piercer or tattooist. Pay attention to his or her appearance. If you're considering a tattoo, ask the tattooist if he or she follows the APT guidelines. (These can be found on page 20.)

Ask yourself if you feel comfortable in the studio.

Ask for references.

Speak with people who have gotten their tattoos or piercings at the shop you visit.

Call your local health department. (The number is listed in the phone book.) Ask about laws regarding tattooing and piercing shops.

Compare prices. (However, do not necessarily be guided by a cheap price.)

Look for an APT, NTA, or APP decal in the window of the shop. Or ask to see if the tattooist or piercer has a certificate from one of these organizations.

Changing Your Mind Is Okay

It is okay to back out of getting a tattoo or piercing. Any reason is all right, even a last-minute one. It's your body, your money, and your decision. You should always know that you can change your mind or wait if you have doubts or feel unsure.

Lauren had visited Kurt at the Cutting Edge studio. She liked what she saw. Everything looked clean. There was an APT certificate on the wall. Kurt seemed friendly and professional. He helped her choose a design. He suggested a black, African tribal design to accent her coppery skin. She made an appointment for a few days later.

In the meantime, Lauren got a temporary tattoo. She put it on her arm and got reactions from her friends and family. Some liked it. Others hated it. Her mom was especially disapproving.

Lauren started having doubts about getting her tattoo. She thought about how she would bleed. Kurt said it would hurt, and she wouldn't be given a painkiller. The tattoo wouldn't come off like mascara. The design might clash with a party dress. If she ever wanted to get rid of it, she'd have to have it lasered off. She could be left with a nasty scar.

She rubbed the temporary tattoo away. Beneath the smear she could see her skin. It looked beautiful just the way it was. She called Kurt and canceled her appointment.

Tattooing and Body Piercing

Points to Consider

Why might a person put a tattoo or piercing where most people couldn't see it?

What are some of the things that might make you uncomfortable during a piercing?

What are some of the things that might make you uncomfortable during a tattooing?

What would you do if you found yourself in an uncomfortable situation with a piercer or tattooist?

How do you think your friends and family would react if you got a tattoo or body piercing? Explain.

Glossary

antiseptic (an-ti-SEP-tik)—substance that kills germs and prevents infection by stopping the growth of germs

autoclave (AW-toh-klayv)—machine that sterilizes equipment

cartilage (KAR-tuh-lij)—a tough connective tissue

flash (FLASH)—tattoo design

henna (HE-nuh)—a reddish brown dye made from the leaves of the henna plant

hepatitis (he-puh-TYE-tiss)—a disease of the liver

HIV (H-I-V)—human immunodeficiency virus; a virus that spreads through body fluids and causes AIDS.

hypoallergenic (hye-po-a-ler-JE-nik)—not likely to cause an allergic reaction

infection (in-FEK-shuhn)—entry of germs into the body; these germs multiply and damage tissue or cause disease.

prejudice (PREJ-uh-diss)—a strong feeling about someone or something; this feeling is formed unfairly or before the person knows the facts.

professional (pruh-FESH-uh-nuhl)—a person who is skilled in a certain field; a qualified expert.

reputable (REP-yuh-tuh-buhl)—having a good reputation; well thought of.

stencil (STEN-suhl)—a single-use, disposable, specially treated paper that transfers a design to the site to be tattooed

sterile (STER-uhl)—free from germs

tetanus (TET-nuhss)—a serious disease caused by bacteria that enter the body, usually through cuts or wounds

For More Information

Fabius, Carine. *Mehndi: The Art of Henna Body Painting.* New York: Three Rivers Press, 1998.

Krakow, Amy. *The Total Tattoo Book.* New York: Warner Books, 1994.

Miller, Jean-Chris. *The Body Art Book: A Complete Guide to Tattoos, Piercings, and Other Body Modifications.* New York: Berkley Books, 1997.

Polhemus, Ted. *Body Art: The Total Guide to Body Decoration.* New York: Element Press, 1999.

Wirths, Claudine G., and Mary Bowman-Kruhm. *Choosing Is Confusing: How to Make Good Choices, Not Bad Guesses.* Palo Alto, CA: CPP Books, 1994.

Useful Addresses and Internet Sites

Alliance of Professional Tattooists
428 Fourth Street, #3
Annapolis, MD 21403
home.safetattoos.com/safetattoos/

American Society for Dermatologic Surgery
930 North Meacham
Shaumberg, IL 60173
1-800-441-2737

Association of Professional Piercers
PMB 286
5446 Peachtree Industrial Boulevard
Chamberlee, GA 30341
www.safepiercing.org/index.html

Childhood and Youth Division
Health and Welfare Canada
9th Floor Jeanne Mance Building
Tunney's Pasture
Ottawa, ON K1A OK9
CANADA

Bodies of Cultures, University of Pennsylvania Museum
www.upenn.edu/museum/Exhibits/bodmodintro.html
Contains gallery of body modification from over the centuries, as well as comments from people on what body art means to them personally and culturally

Virtual Hospital: Iowa Health Book
www.vh.org/Patients/IHB/Derm/Tattoo/
Provides history of body art, questions for people considering body modification, and links

ZoneInn, Vermont Online Youth for Youth Community Network
www.zoneinn.org/phat.html#bodyart
Offers teen views on body art and comments from tattoo and body piercing artists

Index

Index continued